LOVE is an Action Verb

A Caregiver's Journey

To Teri
Some gifts
are unexpected
you are such
a gift

Melodie Yates

We simply cannot do
this alone.

Melodie Yates
April 2024

©2024 Melodie Yates
Love is an Action Verb – *A Caregivers Journey*

eBook ISBN: 978-1-962570-34-3
Paperback ISBN: 978-1-962570-35-0
Hardcover ISBN: 978-1-962570-36-7
Ingram Spark ISBN: 978-1-962570-37-4
Library of Congress Control Number: 2024904158

Editor: Kim Douglas & Janice Nelson
Writing Workshop: Write to Unite
Cover Design: Angie Ayala
Photographer: Jeani Brachbill
Cover and Interior Images: Tammy Kazazi
Interior Design: Marigold2k
Publisher:Spotlight Publishing House™
https://SpotlightPublishingHouse.com

Endorsements

This collection of thoughts, poems and cries from the heart is a precious contribution to collective human experience. Having had the privilege of knowing both Drs Richard & Melodie Yates, reading these poems brought grief of loss and joy of witnessing human love & fortitude. Here we are brought face to face with how two souls live their connected lives, surmounting obstacles of physicality and emerging triumphant spiritually. This triumph is not observed by a materialist age who only celebrates youth and physical health. This is about the messy business of living with a transcendent outlook. I am certain this work will bring some degree of resonance and peace to those in similar situations.

—Farid Sabet, MD
Medical director of Behavioral Medicine Solutions

It probably does not come as a surprise that medical illnesses such as Cancer, Systemic Lupus, Migraine headaches and many others have engendered poetry. Alzheimer's disease, and it is a disease, is no exception but its poetry is more heavily weighted towards caregivers rather than the person's whose brain is affected as they descend into chaos and slowly lose our most precious possession – our identity.

Therein lies the true pain and pathos of Alzheimer's disease; not a physical pain, but something closer to caregiver existential angst, mixed with a large dose of determination, alternating at times with a sense of impending helplessness.

Melodie Yates' volume, *Love is an Action Verb: A Caregiver's Journey*, is an astute and loving tribute to her life partner and husband Richard Yates.

It documents the meandering and varying path that is Alzheimer's disease. Paired with ideas for discussion, it reaches deep into our hearts, the place where feelings lead to new insights and novel approaches to the care of a person with Alzheimer's disease.

—Alan J. Lerner, MD
Neurological Institute endowed chair in memory and cognition
University Hospitals Cleveland Medical Center
Professor of Neurology
Case Western Reserve University School of Medicine
October 2023

LOVE is an Action Verb

A Caregiver's Journey

Melodie Yates

SPOTLIGHT
PUBLISHING HOUSE

Goodyear, Arizona

Contents

Dedication

How does one write a dedication, when in fact, everyone in your life plus all the experiences in your life combine to make you who you are and what you are able to do?

Fundamentally, this book of poems is dedicated to my beloved husband, Richard Yates, without whom these poems would not have emerged. His love and support through our many years of marriage made it possible for me to dig deep enough to do the caregiving needed. The strength gathered through our love for Bahá'u'lláh, the manifestation of God for this day, and the love of our Baháí community has been essential. Surrounded by love given freely by Charlene, Christine, Aaron and Tammy, Nathaniel and Elissa, Ryan and Megan, created space beyond mere survival to sustainability.

And all the others from our extended family of the Warrens and the Williams' who have stood by us each step of the way, to my chosen sisters: Pat, Em, Yvonne, Lily, Margaret, Ruth, Lisa, Debbie and, and, and....

And to the Dementia Caregivers Support Group who embraced me, let me share some of my poetry and confirmed that I wasn't alone. The University Hospital Brain Health and Memory Center team with Dr. Alan Lerner, held our hands and kept Dick healthy and safe for a very long time. They recognized the need for caregiver support and created ways to do just that!

The list would not be complete without mention of my fellow Write to Unite sojourners, supporting each other under the loving, supportive eye of our guide and mentor, Kim Douglas. Of supreme importance is the appreciation and gratitude I feel for the team of caregivers who are selflessly providing aid to my beloved as he resides in 1S at McGregor. One final dedication is for all the caregivers, known and unknown, who are giving, sacrificing, and manifesting love as an action verb.

Foreword

In the vast landscape of human experiences, few journeys are as challenging and poignant as the role of a caregiver for someone with dementia. Each step along this path is fraught with emotional turbulence as caregivers must navigate the ever-shifting contours of their loved one's mind. The complexity of this role is a constant reminder that the human psyche can be as intricate as the most labyrinthine of mazes. Through her profound compassion, courage, and a deep understanding of the caregiver's journey, author Melodie Yates introduces us to this beautiful collection of poetry, a poignant exploration of caregiving for those with dementia.

As a clinical health psychologist specializing in dementia care for three decades, I have witnessed the raw emotions, the unwavering dedication, and the intricate dance of love and loss encompassing the caregiving experience. I first met the author of this remarkable collection, during my time running a Dementia Caregiver Support group. Through our interactions, I came to appreciate her unwavering commitment to her loved one and her remarkable talent for articulating the complex emotions and experiences of dementia caregiving through her poems.

To travel into the unknown recesses of dementia is to confront the stark reality of losing someone you hold dear before they are physically gone. It is a journey that defies conventional notions of time, space, and identity. The poems within this collection delicately articulate the bittersweet experience of witnessing a loved one's transformation as they traverse the uncharted territories of memory loss and cognitive decline. They capture the paradox of holding onto the essence of the person you cherish, even as the relationship slips away, like sand through the fingers.

Through her firsthand experience as a caregiver and her innate poetic sensibility, Melodie Yates brings forth a collection of poems that resonates deeply with those who have embarked on a similar journey. In her words, caregivers will find their own thoughts and emotions mirrored, offering solace and validation during the tumultuous caregiving experience. Melodie's poems provide a beacon of hope amid the darkness, a gentle reminder that they are not alone in their struggles.

Love is an Action Verb: A Caregiver's Journey invites the reader to find solace and understanding as they travel this unchartered journey. These poems provide hope amid the darkness, allowing caregivers to see their reflection within the verses. Through the power of poetic expression, the author offers a lifeline, extending a hand to fellow caregivers and embracing them with validation and empathy. These verses compassionately illuminate the multifaceted nature of the caregiving experience, bringing to light the profound emotional, psychological, and even physical challenges faced by those in this role.

But beyond its empathetic embrace, this collection serves as a guidebook for self-discovery. The poems within these pages invite one to explore the depth of oneself and discover reservoirs of resilience and strength that may have remained hidden. As we delve into the verses, we are reminded that in the face of adversity, love can be a powerful force that propels us forward, even when the path ahead is obscured.

This poetry collection is a testament to the enduring bond between caregiver and loved one, transcending the boundaries of memory and time. It is a tribute to the unwavering devotion of those who courageously shoulder the responsibility and love of caring for someone with dementia. As we immerse ourselves in these verses, we are reminded that within the intricate tapestry of caregiving, there is profound beauty to be found amidst the challenges.

May this poetry collection be a source of solace, inspiration, and self-discovery for caregivers worldwide. Through the raw expression of emotions and compassionate understanding with which each word was crafted, may it illuminate the path and offer a sanctuary of hope, reminding us of all that within the depths of caregiving lies the potential to know the true depth of ourselves.

Lori Stevic-Rust, PhD ABPP
Clinical Health Psychologist
Dementia Thought Leader, Holistic Dementia Care®

Preface

Before I start, I need to share!! My writing mentor and guide asked me, 'What is the divine calling you to do? What is the divine purpose of this work?' This is my answer, maybe my introduction, and most certainly a description of why I wrote my poems. In the moment, did they have some lofty purpose beyond survival? Most certainly not! Upon reflection, though, I can see a greater purpose and reason to invite others on our journey.

My heart says this will help others. What does my soul say? It says that there is more room out than in. Rather than becoming full of resentment and anger, writing poetry was a tool for spilling out frustration, loss, loneliness, and sorrow. It was an exploration of feelings, and through that, I found connection with the divine which led to finding solace. All of this makes room for an overarching love and compassion, honor and commitment—a cleansing, so to speak.

It's the simple day-to-day, week-to-week, month-to-month, year-to-year struggle of caregiving, of love giving. At its core, it is fundamental to the divine—giving sacrificially, giving with love. No big deal on the surface.

No fireworks, no celebratory music, just one person loving another, enough to disappear in the process of giving your all to them. Keeping *just* enough of yourself to recapture it when needed and re-emerge anew when there's time.

The message is personal, and to share it with others may be presumptuous, but it seems like the right thing to do anyway. Humble before God, humble before all of you!!

EGO SPEAK:

A bit of seeking confirmation that all of this is ok, is valid—and that I'm not crazy. And perhaps help others answer that question for themselves!

Introduction

And So It Begins

How does one become a caregiver? It doesn't just jump fully formed into your life, it starts small and then grows with the needs, the changes, the requirements of the moment. Who knew what was going to happen in the ensuing years after my husband's preliminary diagnosis of mild cognitive dysfunction in 2006 on to the formal diagnosis of Alzheimer's disease in 2008. I stood with trepidation not knowing what's next, what the pace of advancement might be of this terminal disease, how long 'normal' might be before.... The following poems were written over the last few years in the caregiving sojourn with my husband at home and beyond to the care facility. They are representative of 16 years of increasingly complex caregiving and demonstrate the range of emotions and experiences, raw and unedited, that poured out of me as I coped with my husband's decline. The journey is not over, and I'm sure there will be more writing to come, but for now, this is enough.

Before I bare my soul and display my vulnerabilities, let me briefly describe the man who has been my husband for 50 years and my closest companion for 50+ years representing more than half of my life; the 'we' that began long before the anguish of Alzheimer's changed the trajectory of our lives together but never our love.

Let me show you Dick. He is an accomplished man, one who was told as a teenager that his destiny was to be the best janitor he could be. This proved to be nothing but a false prophecy as he went on to become a teacher, role-model, warrior against injustice, a champion of humanity. How did he do it? Hard work, determination, support from others, and a few blessings arriving right on time! He earned a BA via a scholarship for the Black male with the highest GPA, surprisingly granted on the last day of high school. That bounty opened opportunities beyond the immediate local prospect of a job at the meat packing plant with his father. He wanted to teach junior high, but his applications were routinely rejected by school districts, boldly stating that 'Negro' teachers were not welcome in 1958 Iowa.

Rather than give up on his aspirations to teach, he left Iowa, moving to Colorado, where he helped lead the struggle to integrate the Denver Public Schools (DPS). While there, he also obtained a master's degree in guidance and counseling and worked as a counselor in a high school. Within a few years, he took up a position at Colorado State University as a college counselor when some of his former students proposed his name after the university claimed that they could not find a Black counselor who would qualify for the position.

His colleagues at Colorado State saw how well he worked with students. Impressed by his skill, they encouraged him to seek a Ph.D. Such an idea represented an undreamt-of possibility for him. Nonetheless, he went on to earn a Ph.D. in counseling psychology from Arizona State University.

He continued to work as a counselor/therapist, eventually becoming the director of the University Counseling and Testing Center at Cleveland State University. Throughout his career, he served in leadership roles, including in a professional organization that certified counseling centers nationally and internationally. He actively contributed to his community serving on boards, earning awards and recognition for his service, and his unwavering commitment to bringing unity forward into reality. He served the Bahá'í Faith, his Faith, with dignity and steadfastness and raised five remarkable children to adulthood and success. His positive impact is mirrored in the countless successes achieved by myriad individuals of all ages and races that he helped in their own journeys.

Before you start:

At the end of each poem is a short explanation about what was going on with me at the time I wrote the poem. This is followed by some reflection questions and an invitation to freewrite. In many ways the poems were my 'freewrite'; they allowed me to release my emotions and clarify my feelings at any given time.

We offer these moments of reflection and release if you want them. These suggestions, prompts, reflections are not as another thing you must do. They are offered with love and here if you want to use them. This is your time — only do what works for you!

Guidelines for Freewriting as described by Sharon Nesbit-Davis

- ♦ Once you begin… keep your hand moving. Don't cross out.
- ♦ Do not worry about spelling, punctuation, grammar.
- ♦ Don't overthink. Don't get logical. Release control.
- ♦ Be courageously truthful.

Ode to the Caregivers

Here's to the Caregivers
whether related or not

Characterized by
Giving when they can
Giving when they can't
Doing as is needed
Doing as is wanted
Doing when it's not
Being there in silence
Being there in repetition

Listening with enthusiasm even
when they know how the story ends

Love is infinite

SAVE SOME FOR YOURSELF!!

Ode to the Caregivers was inspired by a caregiver's support group that helped sustain me in the journey of caring for my husband, Dick.

Journal Question

Reread the poem and select a passage that resonates with you today. Jot the passage at the top of a page in your Caregiver's Journal. Take 2-3 minutes to free-write about this passage and why it resonates with you.

Discussion Questions

What support do you have?
How do you sustain yourself?
How do you care for and love yourself?

Prayer or Passage:

"If I love myself, I love you.
If I love you, I love myself."
~ Rumi.

Don't Borrow Trouble

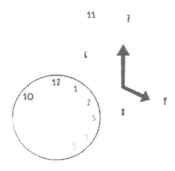

I had planned to write of my beloved husband's increasingly challenging struggle with confusion and understanding and to lament what is coming

a pattern I'd fallen into.

Always what you need arrives when you need it most!

I open a book and read

> *I refuse to borrow tomorrow's troubles and I think that is the way to live. To not suffer before the time comes is a wonderful saving. So many people go through a thing twice — once in anticipation and then in actuality, no sir! Not for me!**

Here it is, plain as day.

And the irony?

Dick is always in real time
not worried about the past,
not worried about the future.

He can only be

in his nanosecond
present

until it
fades

into the next nanosecond.

Please, God
help me be in that nanosecond world
as he needs me to be…

* Excerpt from a letter to May and Sutherland Maxwell
from Rúhíyyih Khánum, April 11, 1939

Don't Borrow Trouble was written as a bit of a cry for relief from the hamster wheel of worry and attempt to control.

Journal Question

It's human nature to worry about the past and the future, to borrow trouble so to speak. How do you talk yourself out of such worries? Take 2-3 minutes to free-write and explore some ideas.

Pick a worry and write about it in a solution-oriented way.

Discussion Questions

When you start to worry, what can you do to refocus?
What kinds of worries can you let go? What worries need solving?

Prayer or Passage

If a problem is fixable, if a situation is such that you can do
something about it, then there is no need to worry.
If it's not fixable, then there is no help in worrying.
There is no benefit in worrying whatsoever.
~ Dalai Lama

Today Was Special

Today was special—my beloved arose in time to join me for prayers

It was blissfully reminiscent of our early days of fasting together

The temptation (prior to my resolution to 'live in the now')
Would be to focus on what is missing between the then and the now
Instead of focusing on the now with joy that

1. He got up and joined me
2. He said a prayer
3. He joined spiritually as I said one of the long fasting prayers

Whoa! The compulsion to assess changes, to identify the deficits, to lament the loss…

IS SO STRONG!!!

Aren't we all a work in progress?

Today was Special was written to capture the joy when it happens and look for it when it's not immediately obvious because joy is always there.

Journal Question

We all have a tendency to focus on what's missing. In this poem, the intention is to focus on finding joy in the moment. Seek the joy and write about it. Take 2-3 minutes to focus on and free-write about a joyous moment.

Discussion Questions

What does joy mean to you?
How can you find joy in the simple moments and pleasures?

Prayer or Passage

Joy gives us wings! In times of joy our strength is more vital, our
intellect keener, and our understanding less clouded.
We seem better able to cope with the world
and to find our sphere of usefulness.
~ 'Abdu'l-Bahá

Balance?

Here's what I wanted to do —
   stay at home with Dick
      and do Nothing....

Push through the cloud of 'overwhelmedness'
threatening to consume me
(and gets me a little every day).

Shoghi Effendi told Sutherland Maxwell
the best way to recover from illness
is to serve the Cause.

Does serving the friends serve as serving the Cause?

I hope so.

I'm feeling better about going to visit friends.

It'll probably be good for me.

I just don't like
making a decision
that in order to ensure

I can go
I must make a decision for Dick
that he can't go when
there's a chance in the moment
he might want to go.

    Sigh!

Experience is showing that the odds are
  he won't want to go
  and/or when he gets there
  he'll want to return home
  shortly after arriving.

Yesterday he came with me to run errands.
He did it. It was great having him with me
But if I'm honest
he was in a fog most of the time
Just following me, waiting
for instructions about what to do next.

What a cruel disease this is!
I must be careful to assess
his capacity with accuracy

versus

letting my own emotional wants interfere.
Or stay trapped in the old family tape:
'push onward regardless of how you feel'
     which trumps
          common sense and compassion every time.

               Hmmmm…. It   seems   I   finally   woke
          up   this morning.

Balance? was written to acknowledge that trudging through the muck has a destination and that the quality of care a caregiver may give is proportional to the ability to put the other person first.

Journal Question

Decision-making can be a hard process for both the caregiver and the individual who needs care. Take 2-3 minutes to focus on and free-write about a moment in your day or week where you found yourself struggling to make a decision.

Discussion Questions

When you have difficulty making a decision, what do you do?
When you get tired of making decisions, what do you do?
Give an example of making a decision when you put the other person first?
How about when you put yourself first?

Prayer or Passage

If you obsess over whether you are making the right decision,
you are basically assuming that the universe will reward you for
one thing and punish you for another…

There is no right or wrong, only a series of possibilities that shift
with each thought, feeling, and action that you experience.
~ Deepak Chopra

Searching the Void Within

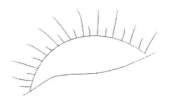

Searching the void within
discovering it's not empty
  but a boxing match
    between
negative self-talk, doubts
    and
affirmations, attributes, virtues

Some days negative wins
A few days positive wins

  Good days offer a shaky
        balance

Personally, I prefer
          the tilt
                toward
                  Light

"Noble have I created thee…
Rise then unto that for which thou wast created." *

You've got your answer, girl.
Extract from Hidden Words of Bahá'u'lláh, Arabic #22

Searching the Void Within helped me understand that if we look beyond ourselves into the divine, there is solace and confirmation there, even when we are enduring a boxing match between our higher and lower nature.

Journal Question

How do you deal with your inner boxing match? Take 2-3 minutes to focus on the struggle between the forces of light and the forces of difficulty.

Discussion Questions

What daily stresses and situations trigger inner negativity and doubts?
What are some ways to transform the negativity into acceptance and neutrality?
What virtues and attributes do we as caregivers cultivate in our journey?

Prayer or Passage

Regardless of what challenge you are facing right now,
know that it has not come to stay.
It has come to pass.
During these times, do what you can with what you have,
and ask for help if needed.
Most importantly, never surrender. Put things in perspective.
Take care of yourself. Find ways to replenish your energy,
strengthen your faith, and fortify yourself from the inside out.
~ Les Brown

Self-love and believing in yourself gives you the power and courage
to change your life.
~ Amanda Ray

The Drip of Decay

It's the little things
    A tuneless hum always in the background
    A joke unshared because it won't be understood
    An intrigue missed on a tv mystery

That expose the big things
    Signs of a destructive disease
    sucking brain function away
    Small irritations in the daily routine

Large swathes of loneliness
            free floating over all that happens

I wrote *Drip of Decay to reveal the long-haul caregiving takes, the power of diseases and the legitimate sadness and loneliness that emerge.*

Journal Question

What are some of the specific details or moments that you live through that reveal the power of the disease or disability of the individual for whom you are caring for? Take 2-3 minutes to focus on and free-write to share these particulars.

Discussion Questions

How do you manage the daily irritations? Loneliness is real in the caretaking journey. What are some ways we can acknowledge and cultivate compassion, and carry ourselves through loneliness to connection?

Prayer or Passage

Loneliness is a wilderness,
but through receiving it as a gift,
accepting it from the hand of God,
and offering it back to him with thanksgiving,
it may become a pathway to holiness,
to glory and to God himself.
~ Elisabeth Elliot

How to Flunk Alzheimer's 101

Number One

    Treat your beloved like all things are normal.

    For example…

        Beloved: Don't exercise on the carpet you'll wear it out.

        Me: That's ridiculous!

        Later in the evening

        Beloved: Are you keeping the fan on all night?

        Me: I'd like to keep it on for a while longer.

        Two second delay, Beloved: Are you keeping the fan on all night?

        Exasperated tone included, Me: I'll turn it off right now!

            And so forth…

Caged by Love

  and responsibility

Surrounded by solitude

alone in making multiple decisions

trapped by the inevitable

  fighting it

  wishing for it

  terrified you might be right -

            things really are getting worse

Number Two

> You say, 'I'll walk a mile in your shoes,' but the reality is that even the most comfortable, empathic shoes wear thin and need to be replaced.

Number Three

Recognition that there is no normal except the normal of abnormal,
  The absence of logic
  Rational thought,
  The irrepressible confusion —
All add up to more than a void, a nothingness
They equal the remains of a loving human being, my beloved, still there with a mind in absentia....

> Now what the heck do you do with that?

Love, love and breathe shallow breaths because the deep ones unearth the emotion buried deep for temporary survival

Logic says breathe deep anyway
> "There's more room out than in...."
> > Something my wise beloved used to say!

Sigh! I'll keep studying harder, I really don't want to flunk.

How to Flunk Alzheimer's 101 was written when I realized how overwhelmed, frustrated, and disappointed I was in myself for displaying the irritation. Writing the poem reminded me that all of us caregivers need to learn to be gentle with our own dear selves.

Journal Questions

Have you found yourself responding emotionally in the moment and then feeling so badly that you lose balance? How can you be gentle with yourself in those moments? What can you say to yourself? Take 2-3 minutes to focus on and free-write to share your insights. How do these questions raise awareness of your emotional needs?

OR

Have you ever found yourself at the end of your rope? What were the circumstances? How did you manage your emotions? What was the aftermath if or when you expressed your feelings?

Discussion Questions

If we're not careful, irritation can turn into resentment. How can we protect ourselves from developing resentments? How can you balance daily irritations by deliberately noticing the moments of joy and gratitude?

Passage or Prayer

Forgiveness is not an occasional act; it is a constant attitude.
~ Martin Luther King Jr.

Resentment is like drinking poison
and then hoping it will kill your enemies.
~ Nelson Mandela

Fine, Fine, Fine

I'm fine — Everything is fine
        Fine

                Fine

                   Fine

A word to describe everything — It means
      That's my answer for if I talk now the emotion is too close to
      the top

      It means — I'm hanging on by a thread

      It means — I'm surviving

      I'm doing what I need to and I'm getting along alright, I suppose

Socially acceptable response
I'm fine speaks volumes

Fine, Fine, Fine was written after answering questions about how my husband was doing, how I was doing. It expresses how if we speak the truth at all times, it may be a bit too exhausting.

Journal Questions

When have you felt like the best way to respond was to just say fine? What were the emotions behind your choice of response? If you could have spoken the truth, what would you have said? Take 2-3 minutes to focus on and free-write to share these particulars.

Discussion Questions

How can we balance truthfulness and vulnerability with the appropriate level of sharing for the setting and situation? What is the expense of letting others in to see our vulnerability?

Passage or Prayer

Honesty and transparency make you vulnerable.
Be honest and transparent anyway.
~ Mother Teresa

Let's tell the truth to people. When people ask, 'How are you?'
have the nerve sometimes to answer truthfully.
~ Maya Angelou

Integrity is telling myself the truth.
And honesty is telling the truth to others.
~ Spencer Johnson

I tried to groan: Help! Help! But the tone that
came out was that of polite conversation.
~ Samuel Beckett

To be wronged is nothing unless you continue to remember it.
~ *Confucius*

Everyone Needs a Margaret*

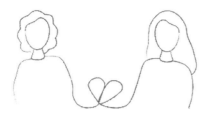

Everyone needs a Margaret, Yvonne, Em, Pat, Lily, Ruth, Lisa, Debbie, Emma, Lori, Harriet, Vince, Amy, Sarah Ann, Barb, Charlene, Christine, Tammy, Elissa, Megan, Aaron, Nathaniel, Ryan…

Who you are

What you do

Is

VITAL

Regardless of title

You are friend, sister, angel

YOU ARE

The warmth in the cold tunnel of loneliness
The stillness in the swirling chaos of daily life
The outreached hand pulling us back to ourselves
The solid foundation on the shaky ground of reality

You do what you do so we can

DO WHAT WE MUST

Trust us when we say you are needed even when we pretend we don't need anyone!!

*Title inspired by Harriet in our Montefiore caregivers' group

Everyone Needs a Margaret was written as a testament to the help we need on the caregiving journey. Whatever illusion we hold that we can do this all by ourselves is just that, an illusion. What a bounty to have those who walk beside us in love and understanding—not to mention literally offering a helping hand!

Journal Questions

When did you recognize that you needed help with caregiving? Maybe you knew from the very beginning. Did you reach out immediately? Resist reaching out? Never reached out? What was the thought process that led to opening up to help and assistance? What barriers, if any, kept you from seeking help? Take 2-3 minutes to focus on and free-write to share these particulars.

Discussion Questions

What societal or cultural messages do we get regarding asking for help or assistance? Do they support or hinder the process of seeking help? How can we as caregivers support each other in reaching out?

Prayer or Passage

Until we can receive with an open heart,
we're never really giving with an open heart.
When we attach judgment to receiving help, we knowingly
or unknowingly attach judgment to giving help.
~ Brené Brown

Where Is...?

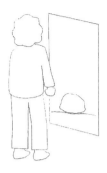

Where is...?
     Invisibility is sought by some
          others not so much.

Look straight at me
     and POOF I'm not there!

          Where is...?
            Fill in the name 'cause the experience is shared by
so many.

I have substance, I have love, I have been here
     Will be here,
          SEE me standing here next to you,
          holding you,
          supporting you,
          inviting you to lean on me!

So, my love, I may be invisible, but I am

SOLID AS A ROCK

Where Is…? was written the first time my husband didn't recognize me. What a gut punch that was. It brought up a bundle of ambiguous feelings of despair while acknowledging the strength that's demonstrated in the continuous process of caregiving.

Journal Questions

Have you had the experience of not being seen by someone dear to you? How did you or would you react? Have you encountered the feeling of being lost? Can you recall how you felt? Take 2-3 minutes to focus on and free-write to capture your reflections.

Discussion Questions

In the course of caregiving, there will be times when we may be reduced to the tasks needing to be done rather than being seen as the person giving the care. How would you cope with that experience? The selflessness required in the caregiving process can be lonely and rewarding at the same time. How do you balance those feelings?

Prayer or Passage

When you are sorrowful look again in your heart,
and you shall see that in truth you are weeping
for that which has been your delight.
~ Kahlil Gibran

I'm Tired

I'm tired of being cold
  though the sun is shining
        brightly

Tired of being lonely
  though I'm surrounded by
        people

I'm tired of being stuck in my head
  though I still have a
        voice

Exhausted by making all the decisions
  though I know what needs
        doing

Tired of feeling inadequate
  though I know I am
        capable

Wearied by the daily struggle
  though I know I'm not
        alone

I'm tired but
  all tests have an ending
  all mountains have a peak

I know with a certainty that I
  lean on God
    lean on family
      lean on friends
        sometimes lean on strangers

And between and through all of it there is rest,
  there is warmth, there is relief, there is

LOVE

Hmm… So what are you complaining about?????

I'm Tired *was a cry for relief, an acknowledgement of the toll it takes. At the same time, it acknowledges the gift of love that is embedded in the process. Sometimes you just need a break anyway!*

Journal Questions

How do you balance the constancy of caregiving with the self-care that is needed to sustain the effort? What have you done to refuel, recharge yourself? Take 2-3 minutes to focus on this aspect of caregiving and free-write to capture your thoughts.

Discussion Question

What support might be needed for caregivers as they do their best to care for their loved one? Describe how love fits into the picture, does it help sustain or detract?

Prayer or Passage

Acknowledging the good that you already have in your life
is the foundation for all abundance.
~Eckhart Tolle

I'm not running away from my responsibilities.
I'm running to them.
There's nothing negative about running away to save your life.
~ Joseph Heller

When? Bit by Bit

When did this happen?
    Bit by Bit
I woke up this morning and realized

I'm caring for an almost invalid.

When did that happen?

    Bit by Bit

First, it's helping with remembering appointments
Doing all the driving
  Making all the decisions

Filling in the blanks for words
    Completing sentences

    Bit by Bit

It's taking out the garbage by yourself
It's doing all the thinking

It's just a little bit here
        And a little bit there

And then you are
   Helping get your Husband out of bed
You're cleaning up accidents
You're helping with showers

   Brushing his teeth

   Bit by Bit

You are up in the middle of the night
    Managing confusion
    Managing un-understood mystery pain

When did this happen?

   Bit by Bit
       With more bits to come…

When? Bit by Bit *describes my growing awareness of the erosion of the independence of my loved one. The increase of dependence upon you can be incremental but no less heavy.*

Journal Questions

When did you discover that the level of caregiving had increased exponentially, but you hadn't noticed? Or perhaps you did notice, what were the emotions attached to that awareness? Take 2-3 minutes to focus on this aspect of caregiving and free-write to capture your thoughts.

Discussion Questions

In what ways can you support yourself and/or others as the journey of decline accelerates? Who are the special people in your life that you can talk to about this, the ones you can ask for help?

Prayer or Passage

It is not the load that breaks you down.
It's the way you carry it.
~ Lena Horne

BAM

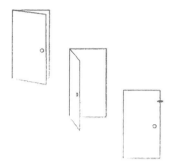

The nature of a door is to
　　　Open and close
　　　　　Sometimes gently sometimes harshly

The open doors in my life are shutting
　　　All at once (not to discount the slow movement
toward the door frames began 15 years ago)

　　　BAM

　　　　　　　Slamming closed with a bang!
Turn to another door —— locked tight

　　　Wait here's another door — shutting too quickly to stick my
foot
　　　　　　　In to keep it open

I didn't recognize the freedom
　　　I had to open the door and go
　　　　　　Walk
　　　　　　Pick up a quick item at the drugstore

Visit a neighbor
Go to a doctor's appointment

You name the goal on the other side of the door… I could go…

Well, my world just shrank to the walls with the doors
            Of our house, our yard

A new door will open — it's promised after all…

Until then I must rely on others
to watch over my precious beloved
who is no longer safe to stay alone for the length of
            a walk, a trip to the drugstore
and … and … and …

Who knew it would be so hard to ask for so much help!

BAM *was written about the shock of realization—your world just shrank in exponential ways.*

Journal Questions

How did it feel to have your world shrink? When did you realize that your independence decreases in direct proportion to the increase in dependency and needs of the person (or people) for whom you were providing care? What was your response? What resources do you have for assistance? Take 2-3 minutes to focus on this aspect of caregiving and free-write to capture your thoughts.

Discussion Questions

Whether participant or observer, how do we reach out to the caregiver whose movement is restricted? Self-sufficiency is highly valued in our society; how do we support ourselves and others to ask for help and to receive assistance?

Prayer or Passage

Regardless of what challenge you are facing right now,
know that it has not come to stay. It has come to pass.
During these times, do what you can with what you have,
and ask for help if needed. Most importantly, never surrender.
Put things in perspective. Take care of yourself.
Find ways to replenish your energy, strengthen your faith,
and fortify yourself from the inside out.
~ Les Brown

Where do I start?

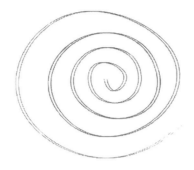

Is it that I'm drowning?
Is it that this journey is
     "Death by 1000 cuts"
Is it that service is the ultimate
     Sacrifice for the one you love?
Is it possible to be all these things?
     To experience all these things:

Yes — I think yes is the answer.

Adjustments to the new normal
That changes so quickly there isn't
Time to catch up…

Two days ago:
     Catching a handful of Tylenol before chewed
     mistaken for candy

Yesterday explaining that yogurt is edible

Today explaining sequence:
    No, you don't go to heaven
    and then you die
    You die and then go to heaven
    Either way there's no coming back.

Placing crumbs in the tunnel of darkness
Doesn't guarantee you can find your way out
Or help your beloved find his way out!

So what do you do?

Just sit in the darkness of the tunnel and
hope someone finds you?

No, the answer is No!

You take your soul's light into that tunnel
And hold his soul's light up so it will be there
when he needs it at the end of this particular journey.

Where do I start? *Thank goodness that all our souls are beyond the infirmities of the body, and we can trust that all that has been lost will be retrieved.*

Journal Questions

What do you do when you feel like you are drowning? Where do you find the light that will lift you out of the water? The divine rests in us all, how do you connect with it and lift yourself and your loved one(s) to that radiant place? Reflect for a few moments and then free-write your thoughts.

Discussion Questions

When you see yourself or others struggling with the weight of caregiving, sliding into depression as they watch the decline of someone they love, how do you support them. What actions can be taken to share the load? Can the load be shared?

Prayer or Passage

It is through gratitude for the present moment
that the spiritual dimension of life opens up.
~ Eckhart Tolle

Putting on a Brave Face
Or
Faking 'til You Make It

Hiding the hollow spaces left by loss
    Of
    Your best friend
    Your
        Intellectual
        Spiritual
        Emotional
            PARTNER

Hollow spaces that echo with their silence
Vibrate with their emptiness
Groan under the weight of the inevitable expansion of

More

H
  A
    L
      L
        O
          W
            S
          P
        A
      C
    E
  S

Can't leave it this bleak
    Need to speak
     Of hope
     Of resilience
     Of ardent swipes that wipe away the dross on the mirror of
my soul
         So that it may shine or maybe shine brighter

But dang, this hurts and I want relief!

What does enough look like?

    I have support
    I have a village
    I have my Faith

I try to let go and let God!
Man, I'm stuck!!

NEWSFLASH!

I've got residual 'letting go issues'

Control issues
Can't survive if I don't do it all myself issues

Some may call it a delusion to think you can do it alone
Others may call it silly

I'd call it reality kicking my behind!
I want to be graceful in my letting go…

I want to be full of gratitude for the blessings embedded in our
life together
And the ongoing micro-joys of our journey to conclusion
undisclosed.

If you are a piece of work,
it means you still have a chance
to find
or make
the rest of the pieces to make you whole!

THANK GOD!

Putting on a Brave Face Or Faking 'til You Make It *was written in a moment of just trying to tell the truth of the feelings and experience of caregiving*

Journal Questions

What are the limits we put on ourselves that keep us from expanding beyond reliance only on ourselves? How can we open up and ask? How can we reach out to others and make this a shared journey? Take 2-3 minutes just to sit quietly and see what surfaces, what answers come and free-write about what you discover.

Discussion Questions

What messages do we get from society about asking for help? Do we create spaces for others to reveal their vulnerabilities safely without judgement? Do we offer help before it's asked of us?

Prayer or Passage

Caregiving often calls us to lean into love we didn't know possible.
~ Tia Walker

There are only four kinds of people in the world:
Those who have been caregivers.
Those who are currently caregivers.
Those who will be caregivers,
and those who will need a caregiver.
~ Rosalyn Carter

When Is Enough E-Nuff?

Is there truly an answer to the question of when is enough E-NUFF?
When…

When do you
    Get extra help?
        Acknowledge that you've been brought
          TO YOUR KNEES!

When do you
        Explore options like care facilities, nursing homes?

Do the bruises on your knees have to bleed?

Does the reflection of yourself in your children's eyes need to be unrecognizable?

When do you
    Accept the inevitability of the conclusion of the disease as it creeps closer, and you can't control it?

When do you
    Admit that the price you are paying for keeping your beloved at home may be too high

For you
  For your family and friends watching you
    For your beloved?

When indeed — I haven't figured it out but I did it anyway —
transitioned my beloved to a
facility…
        and now
              despair
              heart ache
              tears
              twinges of relief

    erosion of control:
              someone else will be responding to his needs — will
it be enough?

        Glimmers of hope that this is a better way
              Despair, heartache, tears, twinges of relief

        GUILT: How could you…
              Who's at home…
              Aren't you sleeping here tonight…
              Where are you going…
              Where's my wife…
              My wife doesn't know where I am…

        Walking, walking, walking the halls trying to get home
        wearing an ankle bracelet to signal nearness to the exit…

What do I do with all of that? I must remember the light
I'm holding for him…
Must convey love, warmth, and safety as I leave him
here in his confusion!
O God! When does certainty emerge that this was
the right choice?

Twinges of relief
        Mixed with despair, heartache and tears

The twinges are getting bigger, stronger
                    BUT
                  I
                AM
                      STILL
                        LOST!!!

When Is Enough E-Nuff? was an acknowledgement that living with the decision to put my husband in a care facility came with a bunch more emotion than ever expected. Who knew it would be the hardest decision ever?

Journal Questions

Have you felt like you can't take anymore? Or that the choices before you are not palatable regardless of the choices? Does the choice you make compete between knowing it's the right one and fearing it may be the wrong one? Take a few minutes to explore and reflect, then do some freewriting about what surfaces.

Discussion Question

When no choice is ideal for the next stage of caregiving, how do you support yourself or others in the decision-making process?

Prayer or Passage

Self-compassion is simply giving the same kindness
to ourselves that we would give to others.
~ Christopher Germer

Breathe.
Let go.
And remind yourself that this very moment
is the only one you know you have for sure.
~ Oprah Winfrey

Who Waits for Me?

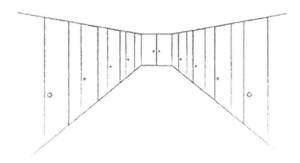

Two big heavy wooden doors
Pulled hard to open,
Two more doors,
Wait for the buzzer,
Then the front desk.
Sign in once, then
Twice to get the key.

I clip a white square card embedded with a code,
Onto my pants, the hidden retractable
String reaches the electronic lock.
No entry without the plastic.

I walk by the majestic fireplace,
Welcoming visitors to a cozy corner,
Down the corridor on the left look up at the edge of the ceiling,
Orange, brown, red leaves all scattered by the wind: Fall
White sparkling snowflakes float: Winter
A robin hovering above a nest on a blooming branch: Spring

A flurry of butterflies: Summer
A reproduction of the famous Four Seasons Stained-Glass Panels
Or a symbol of the endless passage of time.

Lower on the right,
Resting on the old-fashioned organ,
Musical notes form Holy, Holy, Holy.
Deep green mosaic tiles
From the shade of an old Tiffany lamp
Light the page.

You can't hear it,
But you can feel it--
Over one hundred years of families, friends, caregivers
Plodding down the wooden hall to their loved ones.

Out comes the plastic, the gateway to opening the elevator,
Inside, another swipe needed to gain entry onto the locked floor.

More steps now on carpet this time,
Muted grey with swirls blend,
Its weaves leave no impression.

The wreath on the door, a spray of pink flowers,
Left there by a previous resident--
No need to remember a room number.
Just look for the wreath.

Marble bench framed by a bay window.
Sunsets seep in daily.
Red spirals, fiery oranges streak across the evening sky.

Long legs wrapped in blankets,
Closely cropped gray stubble sprinkled on a balding head,
Chin lolls on his chest.
Glasses slipping down his nose.

Dark brown skin exposed at the side of the covers,
Golden brown eyes look up,
And he smiles.

I'm recognized,
Still remembered as wife.

Postscript
Every visit to my beloved takes me down that hall.
Who came before?
How long will I walk this corridor?
Who waits for me each visit?
His soul is the same.
His physical essence fades in small ways every day.

Who Waits for Me? *was written as a reflection of what it is like to walk down the hall to get to my beloved and the unknown that waits for me when I visit.*

Journal Questions

As you care for your loved one, what do you see, hear, smell? What details do you notice in the environment? How can you honor yourself by describing the changes where your loved one resides? What glimpses of your loved one remain the same? Can you frame the difficult changes with love in a way that honors the passage of time? How do your beliefs, whether spiritual or not, help you accept the changes that are occurring? How do we pause to allow peace and understanding to replace the tumult? Take a few minutes to explore and reflect, then do some free-writing about what surfaces.

Discussion Questions

How do we cope with the long haul of caregiving that allows compassion for our loved ones and ourselves? When confronted with a new challenge or new twist in the caregiving routine, how do we manage? What is the value of slowing down in that moment to reflect and regroup?

Prayer or Passage

If you can't fly then run, if you can't run then walk,
if you can't walk then crawl,
but whatever you do,
you have to keep moving forward.
~ Rev. Martin Luther King, Jr.

Cleaning Out the Files

Need a trip down memory lane?

A life well lived
    A life forgotten
A life well loved
    A life forgotten

Honey, did we…

A life drilled down to the basics
    Use the spoon for your soup
        Which one is the spoon?
            I point out this as he picks up a cup

Cleaning out the files that have no use no place anymore

A life forgotten though well filled
    With purpose, love, service,
    dedication to God and humanity.

The evidence is in our memories, in the treasuries of our hearts
    Not locked in a file cabinet of a body full of empty files
But rather in the untouched soul glorious in its beauty and nobility.

Cleaning Out the Files *described how truth and hope wrap together in survival.*

Journal Questions

Have you ever been stumped or overwhelmed by the feeling of loss? What have you done to lift yourself up and out? Can you see the light? Can you feel the treasures hidden in the absence of someone else's lost memories? Take a few minutes to explore and reflect then do some freewriting about what you are feeling.

Discussion Questions

How do you lift up someone or yourself as they/you confront the truth of what is gone, what remains? Is there another framework besides loss? What might that framework look like?

Prayer or Passage

Kindness can transform
someone's dark moment
with a blaze of light.
You'll never know how much your caring matters.
~ Amy Leigh Mercree

Let me reassure you that you can rejuvenate & heal yourself on all levels simply by beginning to look at things, situations, places & people from a newer perspective & by committing to let go of the thoughts, behaviors & feelings that keep you from being your best.
~ Rajesh Goyal

Holding Two Realities

BALANCE

Between the gut punches of

    "Who are you?"

    "Where is my wife?"

While simultaneously relying on God
Trying to be grateful for the bounties
Embedded in the cracks and canyons

The bleakness of the journey counterbalanced
By the joy, love and thankfulness for every year, every
moment together

BALANCE

The dueling realities fighting for supremacy—
No worries
Reliance on God wins every time!!!

Holding Two Realities *was a distillation of the hardest and simplest task around — reliance on God.*

Journal Questions

Who do you turn to when your tank is completely empty? Is it the Divine in whatever form or a person? Who or what do you rely on to get you through? If the answer is nothing/no one, how do you change that so there is something greater than yourself to give you nourishment and sustenance? Take a few minutes to reflect and free-write what stands out to you.

Discussion Questions

Whether it is reliance on God or some other source of strength, can you or those you support flourish without reaching beyond themselves? Where do they turn? What hand might you have reaching for them?

Prayer or Passage

My fortress was My reliance on God,
and My shield Mine attachment to that peerless Friend;
Mine armour was Mine unfailing trust in Him,
and My hosts Mine ardent hope in His grace.
~ Bahá'u'lláh

Can You Be Whole with a Hole?

Yesterday I realized I'm not really whole.

Today I realized a reason why…

I have a hole. I would imagine it's like a missing limb,
    Except it is
               INVISIBLE
    To the naked eye

It is visible to the discerning eye though

The hole shows up
    By noticing the look of sadness
        The   half   enthusiastic   engagement   in
conversation
It shows in the lethargy of my daily existence
    The cringes of a sudden "phantom limb" pain.

Whoa — that's exactly what it is, my own phantom limb!

I want to be on a journey toward wholeness
To fill in the hole with a new perspective
        Or recognition of, or embracement of the
                PROCESS

Losing my partner, my lover, my best, most trusted
companion
While he still breathes creates an amputation of sorts in
real time
        There's grief but no closure....

I'm curious — what does the prosthesis look like?

Can You Be Whole with a Hole? *Again, speaking a truth, a hurt, a reality within the moment, a less than satisfactory solution.*

Journal Questions

Do you ever dwell on the missing, the loneliness, the absence of what was once there? And if you do, how do you bring yourself back out of that 'hole'? Where do you find the light? Take a few minutes, what do you feel, what do you see? Free-write and read what you discover.

Discussion Questions

Where does one get emotional therapy for living with a 'phantom limb'? Is it through the support of friends and family? Support groups? Truth-telling and truth-facing?

Prayer or Passage

The risk of love is loss, and the price of loss is grief –
But the pain of grief is only a shadow
when compared with the pain of never risking love.
~ Hillary Stanton Zunin

You cannot prevent the birds of sorrow from flying over your
head, but you can prevent them from building nests in your hair.
~ Old Chinese proverb

More Room Out Than In

Sounds churning inside me
Emotions upspoken anchored in my gut
Destructively seeping into my muscles, bones and organs
To re-emerge as disease, dysfunction formed from crystalized toxins.

Is it grief?
    pain?
      anguish?

Resentment?
    Abandonment?

Whatever it is requires space to resolve to evolve
into an expression of emotion that needs release
      to find true peace.

LET IT
    LET THEM
        OUT!

More Room Out Than In. *Growth, release — it all comes from making room for the good stuff and getting rid of the bad stuff*

Journal Questions

Sometimes the fear of letting go is stronger than the compulsion to keep stuffing the feelings into myself. Is that an experience you share? How do you find balance? How do you let go so that your body doesn't carry the unnecessary, the need to control the uncontrollable? Do your own search and acknowledgment for what works, what might work for you. Take a few moments to reflect and then free-write what comes up or, more importantly, what comes out!!

Discussion Questions

More room out than in — easy enough concept, hard to put into action. What does support look like for those stuck, those who are so full with the grief or the circumstances, to make room for their body and mind to breathe? How does the village support each other?

Prayer or Passage

But feelings can't be ignored,
no matter how unjust or ungrateful they seem.
~ Anne Frank

Care for your psyche... know thyself, for once we know ourselves,
we may learn how to care for ourselves.
~ Socrates

I learned that courage was not the absence of fear,
but the triumph over it.
The brave man is not he who does not feel afraid,
but he who conquers that fear.
~ Nelson Mandela

What Does Recovery Look Like?

What does recovery look like?
I say I'm in burnt out recovery
  Maybe that's the wrong direction
    A misguided sentiment

Maybe what I really need to do is not try
    To recapture who I used to be
But to embrace the possibilities of
Who I can become now…in this new reality.

Who do I want to be now?
        Still a wife, mother, caregiver
        Woman of courage
          Of substance
          Of wisdom
          Of generosity

Reestablish or recognize anew
            My inherent nobility?

Stop worrying about who I was and celebrate
    THE YOU THAT'S NOW?

Or better yet,
    Shape the me
        I want to be!

What Does Recovery Look Like *Searching for what's believed to be lost only to discover that it was always there being polished for the 'big reveal'!*

Journal Questions

Losing yourself is not uncommon in the caregiving journey. How do you maintain balance? What does the 'recuperation' process look like as the journey changes and evolves? If you look back at the 'who you were' then to the 'who you are' now, what does that look like? Take a few moments to find your story, free-write it and see what it says.

Discussion Questions

Who are you? Who were you? How do you help yourself or others to answer those questions? What are the benefits to acknowledging the changes we go through as caregivers? How do we best support that process or nurture a positive resolution?

Prayer or Passage

Our physical, emotional, and spiritual health requires rest.
We need to take a break.
We need to nurture ourselves.
To take a time out to refuel, rejuvenate, and revive ourselves.
~ Dana Arcuri

You cannot swim for new horizons
until you have courage to lose sight of the shore.
~ William Faulkner

Force of Nature

Shall I claim it?
        Being a force of nature.

If I do,
    is that ego?

    Or just a fact-check
    amid life's reflections?

This notion came to me - insight blooming
flashing streams of confirming energy
Connecting dots from childhood 'til now.

My survival
    My self-engineered rising above,
            Beyond the trauma

      My triumph over adversity to marry and flourish

        My continuing caregiving of my loving husband

My dissolving
    Evolving
        Emerging self

Requires a force of nature

And nature comes from God
    So, it follows that
God was and is the instrument behind
    My strength
        My survival
            My life
                And all its bounties, challenges, and realities

So, hush, my precious one, you are exactly as intended:

A noble, beautiful force of nature!!!

A Force of Nature *is a celebration of the spirit, triumph of the soul, hope for the future.*

Journal Questions

How do we acknowledge our power and emotional resilience? Does society allow us to celebrate who we are, and the distance traveled in this caregiving journey? How do you recognize the hand of the Divine in the twists and turns on this path of life that includes caring for a loved one? Take a few minutes to reflect, and acknowledge the learning, the trials, and the triumphs you've traversed. Free-write the results and celebrate your successes. Embrace yourself!

Discussion Questions

How often do we pause to reflect on the positive, on the achievements in the course of caregiving? What sustains us? What inner strength is in evidence—either for ourselves or the ones we support? When do we shine a light on the resilience, perseverance, and strength it takes, or has taken, to be of service to our loved ones?

Prayer or Passage

Our way is not soft grass; it's a mountain path with lots of rocks.
But it goes upwards, forward, toward the sun.
~ Ruth Westheimer

Everything you need is within you,
the strength, courage and confidence to change your life.
You just need to look within yourself and find it.
~ Amanda Ray

About the Author

University administrator turned author, Dr. Melodie Yates, served 40+ years in higher education teaching, conducting research and training students, faculty, and staff competencies related to diversity, inclusion and belonging. Now age 74, Melodie is a survivor (you can read about details in her next book, *I've Climbed Invisible Mountains*).

Married for 50 years to an amazing man, who for the last 16 years has progressed deeper into his Alzheimer's disease, she wrote poems as a release. They were a means of letting off steam, naming and claiming her frustration and emotions as they came.

Her related credentials are flexibility, love, perseverance, and desperation. With no formal training in writing, no particular expertise in caregiving beyond learned experience, she hopes by sharing her journey, others will find solace and confirmation.

Through the Write to Unite Program, led by Kim Douglas, Melodie has been able to create *Love is an Action Verb: A Caregiver's Journey*. These poems and their accompanying reflections are a piece of the author's soul. Join her to experience the validity of our interconnectedness.

Made in United States
Orlando, FL
12 April 2024